Gratitude

Ariele M. Huff

Copyright © 2016 Ariele M. Huff

All rights reserved.

ISBN-10: 1534737693
ISBN-13: 978-1534737693

DEDICATION

To Brad

CONTENTS

	Introduction	i
1	Gratitude: Never Wasted Time	3
2	Giving Thanks	5
3	Thanksgiving excerpt	7
4	Gammy Gaston's Okra Gump	10
5	Joyous Ruminations	12
6	Dramma and Drappa	14
7	I Love You	18
8	Thank You	19
9	Thanks Given to Me	26

INTRODUCTION

Ways to express gratitude, reasons for doing it, and the wonderful outcomes of doing it are presented in this little book to give readers ideas to build a gratitude practice or simply to enjoy life more —few things are so satisfying as to relax back into thoughts of all those who have done right by you!

GRATITUDE: Never Wasted Time!

When I was first with my husband, I noticed he did an unusual thing. He frequently told me and many other people how much he appreciated things. He didn't wait for the really big gift or the heroic effort to say thanks. Appreciation and gratitude were continually on his lips.

I had to step back from this at one point and decide if it irritated me or not; it was that unusual an experience in my life. Did I find it aggravating to be stopped as I carried a load of laundry to the washer and be thanked for doing so? Isn't it over the top to hear how much Brad appreciates what a lovely home we have each time he steps in the door? Do other spouses really thank each other for a kiss or a hug?

My first reaction was confusion: What did he want? On reflection, that seemed clear— more of the same. My next reaction was to wonder if my husband was so continuously complimentary because he was weak. Were these unctuous requests for my approval and continued love/service/expenditures? If that was the case, why were there never recriminations when he didn't get a proof of love? If he was weak, why didn't he seem weak?

At this point, I began to wonder how any person could afford just to drop these compliments like so many lovely flowery, lace-edged valentines clearly with no expectation or need for their return. After all, I had seen him leave a sweet word with a cashier who was friendly, a stranger in the parking lot who was returning shopping carts to the store, a neighbor whose small garden was nice but not spectacular. Didn't this effusion of appreciation deplete some hidden resource within my mate? Wouldn't he run out, probably exactly when he needed extra reserves most? Even as I thought this, it seemed ludicrous. There were no signs of running out. In fact, these numerous verbal gifts seem to leave Brad revitalized.

My process of observation netted me these conclusions: Expressing gratitude at every opportunity without any expectation of return makes other people feel good, it feels good to the person doing it, it doesn't seem to annoy anyone, it sometimes provides a return, it does not drain a limited resource, and it is not a sign of weakness.

Hmmm, I said to myself, maybe I should try it. So I tried it tentatively at first, and I was observant of the response I got and how I felt. Was I creating an expectation of more expressions of gratitude that would be onerous to fulfill? Not if I only did it when I wanted to. Did it feel insincere? Not if I was sincere. Did it feel like a waste of time? No, it felt like an easy thing to do, and it didn't require any time I wasn't already utilizing interacting with someone. Would people think I was strange because I was showing gratitude for something most people wouldn't mention? Although I have gotten some curious looks, it seems everybody likes to be acknowledged.

After an initial period of testing, I became more comfortable giving recognition to others for their laudable behaviors, whether small or large. And I also began to express gratitude, as my husband does, to the Universe in general for warm sunshine, a beautiful snowfall, an unexpected flower along the roadside, the purr of a cat, a day-off from work, a good day at work.

Finally, I even began to be openly thankful for the value of a difficult experience: the lesson learned on a tough day at work, the important message brought by a physical injury, the necessary information delivered by an argument or confrontation.

What else is there to say? Thanks for listening. And thanks, Brad, I appreciate what you taught me, and I'm grateful you are in my life. Published 11/95 in *The New Times*

GIVING THANKS

Long before Oprah had attained wealth and success, even before she'd charmed us with her role in *The Color Purple*, I was writing gratitude journals—and calling them "Good Things Lists."

You're right—"Gratitude Journal" is a better name, but my lists are very powerful for me. I do them especially when things really seem bleak, and they worked, and continue to work, for me.

Unlike Oprah's concept, my lists are done and completed when needed and don't require "five things to be grateful for each day" in the kind of ongoing journal format that is daunting to many people. Instead, my lists cover everything I can conjure up that is or was or will be beneficial in my life. For example, I never fail to mention anything that is right with my health, finances, family, or career. I also include those entities whose welfare affects me: "healthy pets" or "Mom recovering well after surgery" or "car only needed a new gasket" or "front bathroom remodel job finally completed."

Also unlike the "Gratitude Journal," my lists do not include general mention of day-to-day pleasures like "good waffles this morning" or "beautiful sunset." My less sibilant name for enumerations like that: "Things I like lists." Those are important too because they help me to make a point of giving myself more enjoyable experiences.

However, my "Good Things Lists" have been dynamic in restoring my faith in myself, in others, in life's process. They put all the reasons for keeping on at keeping on right in front of my face as inarguable evidence that my efforts are worth continuing, that I do have some luck and successes. This works for me every time, even though, there are always some entries reflecting less than perfect conditions: car still running, Fluffy maintaining on daily insulin, income improved.

I believe that one of the values of my lists is that they don't ignore problems, responsibilities, or necessary work to be done. They present a realistic but hopeful view of my life at any given time. And...they have always made me feel better, whether I'm struggling with illness or relationship conflicts or financial insecurity or emotional issues like fear, sadness, and anger.

My writing exercise for you, my readers, is to create a "Good Things List." (This form of giving thanks is as great a "preventative" of ills as it is a rescuer in tough times.) Then, post the list somewhere it can be seen as you go about your daily tasks.

Let me know if you notice a change in your perception of how good life is. Please send 200 words or less. You can contact me through my website: http://arielewriter.myfreesites.net or at my writers blog: http://wirterswingsbyariele.blogspot.com OR contact me by email at ariele@comcast.net.

Published in *Northwest Prime Time's* Writing Corner 11/2002

The Queen of Mean:
The Conversion of a Cold and Prejudiced Heart
[Thanksgiving Excerpt]

Thanksgiving: Shirley and Bernadine had set four foldout tables down the center of Shirley's long living room. Every year for the last ten years, Shirley had invited fifteen to twenty immigrants and refugees to join her family in their Thanksgiving celebration.

"It's one of the loveliest parts of American culture, and I enjoy sharing it with those who haven't experienced it," she had explained to Bernadine when presenting her with an invitation to come and help.

"Every year we have more people, and I can't handle it by myself anymore." Shirley didn't say she knew Bernadine would be alone, had been alone every holiday for years. Her Thanksgiving parties were not just a time to share her American culture but were also a time when she learned more about her guests' cultures than she did all year long at her reception desk where she dealt with over a hundred people every week. This year—for the first time, Bernadine seemed both interested in and worthy of inclusion.

The tables groaned with food contributions from everyone: turkey and dressing snuggled between humus with pita bread and eggrolls; couscous and peanut sauce shared a tablecloth with a huge pan of spanakopita; tamales and hum bao circled a plate of sushi with umeboshi plums. Bernadine's pecan/pumpkin double-decker strata pie was side-by-side with baklava and apple strudel.

Dinner was a tower of Babel affair. Bernadine sat between Ivetta and Misbah. She learned at least five different ways to say "pass the gravy." She learned there are many ways to wrap a sari, that the Black Sea is in the Ukraine, and that meals have many courses in Moscow.

While stomach space for dessert was developing, the general conversation turned to reasons for being thankful. One after another the group took the floor to share reasons for gratitude. Lin was grateful her family was still alive in spite of the attack by pirates as their boat made its way to freedom. At twelve, Lin had been raped and had watched as others were raped, robbed, and killed.

Vasiley was appreciative because he no longer was the object of persecution based on his black curly hair, dark eyes, and porcelain white skin. In his country, he had run from beatings by vigilante groups more than one time.

Joyce Chan was glad she was making enough money to send back home to support an uncle in prison. She said it took every extra cent to bribe guards to feed and not to beat her relative.

Mahmoda was thankful for an opportunity to go to school. In her country, women were seldom even taught to read. She could not read in her native tongue.

Then it was Bernadine's turn. What could she say? The other stories made her white hot aware of her reasons to be grateful, but where was her pain that could be compared to these harrowing stories? As she looked from one waiting face to the next, it dawned on Bernadine with the glare of a noonday sun erupting over the eastern horizon. Her pain, her loneliness, was clear, but not to be admitted…not then, not there.

In consternation, Bernadine began to drop tears, and once the storm cloud was seeded, it burst. A bouquet of culturally appropriate responses hovered around, across, and over her: Asians averted their eyes and bowed their heads in silent empathy; Hispanics and Russians laid hands and arms on her; a Norwegian slapped her heartily on the back as though Heimliching the sobs right out of her would work. A shower of foreign expressions of sympathy cascaded over Bernadine's head and washed through her like a soothing rain, coated her like a lava flow of love.

The pitter patter of hands stroked and brushed against Brigit beneath Bernadine's cardigan sleeve, and then they, or she, decided it was time to get closer. The sleeve drooped and slid to the elbow. One by one the clutch of comforters spied the arm and fell back into a circle of gawkers. Only a few of their cultures approved of such body art, on women. Nor were they used to seeing American women of Bernadine's kind decorated in such an elaborate way.

"Well," Lorena gave her best full-throated importance to the vowel, "you are a craysee girl." Admiration vibrated through her voice and shone from her biased eyes. She extended a finger and poked Brigit in the nose, causing her to take on a wry and puckered expression.

"I like it velly much," Setsuko intoned gravely.

"Very much, very nice," repeated several voices politely.

It might have been Misbah who started the tittering or Joyce who was suppressing a grin behind her hand, and it certainly was Ivetta who began belly laughing and Vasiley who joined her, followed quickly by Maria and Thanh. At any rate, it was probably not Shirley who started it, but everyone, including Bernadine finished it.

Bernadine sank into sleep like a pebble thrown into soft snow. She found herself gazing into the mysterious, crystalline interior of a glacier's snout. A glacial pool reflected the white and blue-edged mass behind it, and cool purple mountains rose into the sky on every side. While Bernadine looked, a light snow began to drift around her, icing the top of the glacier. This is me, Bernadine thought. This is like the way I've been for years: so cold and so lonely. This is like me.

Immediately, a wind surged into the stillness, and Bernadine was blown and swept into a forest where a drenching rain was falling. Lightning and thunder crashed and flickered. A tree nearby was split and blackened to the undergrowth. The rain pelted mercilessly. No, this is me, Bernadine thought. This is like the confusion and upsetting feelings I've been having for months: the confrontations and angry outbursts.

As soon as she thought it, the rain slacked and diminished, and Bernadine found herself looking at a shimmering double rainbow, its ends overlapping. As she continued to watch, the sun brightened, and Bernadine could feel its warmth on her back and head. She felt herself crying with joy and relief. No, this is me, she thought. This is me now: generous and kind, with friends for conversation and companionship. This is me now.

The warmth of the sun penetrated her, and Bernadine awoke feeling relaxed and happy.

eBook link: http://www.amazon.com/dp/B00TMCFPBG
Paperback: http://www.amazon.com/dp/1511538899

GAMMY GASTON'S OKRA GUMP

A housewife in the fifties, my mother had degrees in Art, English, and Education, which mainly made her appear to her in-laws as highly over-qualified for the job. She cheerily relinquished her career as an innovative teacher and turned to making intricate Shakespearean dioramas and St. Patrick's Day shadow silhouettes for her two bickering daughters and our high school-educated father.

No one could surpass my mother in transforming a mundane after school snack or minor holiday into an art project of elaborate dimensions. Returning home with our red plaid lunch boxes, my sister and I might find the kitchen table covered by a replica of a tiny skating party complete with icy pond, sparkling angel hair snow drifts, and snowsuit clad babies building snowmen. Appropriate refreshments—hot cocoa and painstakingly authentic Lebkuchen—were waiting and a carefully chosen segment from *Hans Brinker and the Silver Skates* was read to us as my sister and I engaged the snow babies in battles that left the powdered sugar ice rink dusting our hair and faces.

None of this fazed my mother the teacher. An energetic optimist, she continued creating costumes, toys, parties, and projects that far outstripped our ability to comprehend the effort or meaning involved.

Only one thing could daunt my mother's classically trained celebration skills: her in-laws' ownership of all large holidays.

My father's gigantic Midwestern blue-collar family caravanned from the Iowa dustbowl to the Northwest where my mother's family was already quietly attending college, the theater, and concerts. Dad was the upstart with philosophical interests, but he wasn't willing to give up the huge family reunions orchestrated for Thanksgiving, Christmas, and the fourth of July.

Her discomfort poorly concealed, my mother sat in rooms with badly decorated Christmas trees, eating some kind of mud-colored rum-soaked dessert as she debated with an in-law about a political, religious, or philosophical issue. She never initiated these confrontations, but rather was a target for the slightly sloshed or brazenly hostile who wanted to prove she wasn't smarter than her adopted family, and who hadn't the wit to see how they were proving the opposite of their point.

Gammy's Okra Gump was the final straw. A vicious old woman, Gammy presented her gump at every holiday meal and was so feared that it was eaten and never spoken of except to imply its traditional permanence, if not its merit.

After an initial sample, Mom tried refusing, accepting but not eating, and a variety of other ineffective solutions. Finally, as the gooey dish was set before her for perhaps the fortieth time, my mother rose, summoned us to the car, and we left gumpless with our holidays reclaimed for fantasy decorations and gourmet feasts. In this, my father was uncharacteristically grateful and cooperative.

Soon afterward, Mom returned to teaching...where she received the respect and gratitude she so richly deserved.

Published in *The New Times*

JOYOUS RUMINATIONS

Daydreaming about positive things helps to create a positive reality. Studies have shown that two things work against us in depression and anxiety. The first is if we have difficulty disputing negative thoughts and beliefs, and the second is if we spend time ruminating on negative things.

It's easy enough to do, isn't it? News stories are slanted toward showing the problems and fearful things, and so are many television programs, movies, magazine articles, and novels. It can be hard to remember the good stuff when we're inundated with the bad.

Of course, nature also abhors a vacuum. So it may be easy to say, "just don't get into circular worrying," but it's another thing simply to wipe those thoughts from the mind.

What works better is to substitute another kind of thinking. (Gardeners know that the best way to deal with weeds is to squeeze them out with desirable plants. This is both more attractive and easier than continuously weeding and leaving the space empty for new unwelcome plants.)

The habit may seem hard to develop at first, especially if you've felt overwhelmed by the pessimism surrounding you and within you. However, the task becomes easier if it's recognized that, at the outset, it may feel contrived to turn thoughts to pleasant things. Once the new enjoyment habit is established, it will seem as natural as the old worrying one. Setting aside a specific "worry time" to contemplate the list of misgivings and to solve problems is a suitable method of containing time expended in this way. Remember to limit this to a specific time of day and to no more than an hour per day.

Some topics to dwell upon for possible joyous ruminations: cooking, eating, decorating seasonally, holidays, romances, school, events, celebrations, tastes, smells, sounds, textures, visuals, recreation, sports, travel, hobbies, shopping, get-togethers, books, epiphanies, nature, pets, neighbors, rewards, awards, accomplishments, gifts, and compliments.

If bad experiences connected to the topic arise, simply remind yourself that this is not your worrying time.

I keep one journal used only for joyous ruminations. Here is a sample of one of mine, though entries vary a lot in format:

"Signs of serenity: 1) stopping to enjoy holiday decorations and seasonal produce with deep breaths of joy and anticipation, 2) watching the ripples I make in the tub reflect lightning bolts from candle glow, 3) smiling at strangers and smoothing situations pleasantly, 4) laughing at pets' funny behaviors, even when what they're doing is messy or inconvenient."

Thanks for the idea of joyous ruminations goes to avid daydreamer Daniel O'Brien of Everett, a member of my Write About Your Life class at the Greenwood Senior Center.

If you need some further help with turning musings in a more affirmative direction, I have a list of "Encouraging Words" and a handout called "Morning Questions." These may trigger cheerful reveries as well. Contact me at ariele@comcast.net.

DRAMMA AND DRAPPA

One of the best reasons for RVing, as we all know, is to visit relatives, who have inconveniently placed themselves too far from the nest. Or perhaps the nest has moved away from them. Either way, an RV makes the commute between Washington and Connecticut or Oregon and Oklahoma a lot less daunting.

Visiting grandkids is about my top favorite travel activity. However, as I've discussed in previous columns, these stopovers can be fraught with interesting challenges. We recently learned a lot during a Christmas over night.

The title of this column comes from our three and a half-year-old grandson. He used to call us Gappa and Pumpkin (my husband's pet name for me), before he'd mastered his "r's." Rowan is my youngest daughter's first child and she is expecting her second.

That was part of the problem. We came as reinforcement grandparents to help at a difficult time. The kids had recently moved across the country and were in the process of beginning to build on a lot while living in a rental house too small for all their possessions. The planning of a second pregnancy at this point, although intentional, clearly was having its arduous ramifications.

When we arrived early on Christmas Eve day, we found my daughter incapacitated with morning sickness that lasted most of the day, our grandson acting out his confusion over the move, and our son-in-law uncharacteristically grumpy and harsh with his wife and child. No food had been prepared, no gifts wrapped, and no decorating done. All these things were understandable, yet awkward. What's a grandparent to do?

My reading about grandparental roles has impressed upon me the importance of not inflicting my ideals on grown children—who already know them anyway. My husband and I quickly analyzed the situation and saw that the best way to ease things for the adults was to remove our misbehaving grandson from right beneath their noses. We did this soon after he'd broken an overhead light fixture by swinging his belt at it.

Fortunately, the day was mild enough for outdoor play. Between the two of us, and our Jack Russell, we shamelessly ran the child ragged, chasing footballs, piling leaves and jumping into them, and that kind of thing. Then we were lucky enough to locate a nearby theater with a screening of *The Emperor's New Groove*. Imagine our delight when we realized we had the theater to ourselves!

Rowan raced up and down the aisles and collected garbage (jarbage) to throw away, until the movie began. He sat in the front row watching the movie in a kind of slack jawed stupor. It will always be one of my favorite Christmas memories.

When we got back to the small rental house, it was pleasantly decorated and filled with smells of my son-in-law's gourmet cooking. My daughter's nausea had abated, and we all spent a memorable Christmas Eve. Our grandson slept between Drappa and Dramma in our guest bed.

Days after we'd left, I was still processing what had happened. My initial impulse when we'd walked into the house was to rush in like the cavalry: cleaning, cooking, and disciplining both my grandson and son-in-law.

However, my guardian angel must have been watching out for me on this particular occasion. My role has changed. This is my family, and yet it is not my nuclear family anymore. My days of being the mother warrior are over, whether I like it or not. (Okay, I pretty much like it.)

To me, this change means my problem solving tools are also

somewhat altered. I remember as a young mother recognizing the value of re-channeling the energies of a disobedient child. I used this strategy often and with success. My early experiences have come in handy now that as a grandma my behavior modification methods are more limited.

The other aspect to this that I only realized fully during this Christmas Eve trip is that a child will usually behave, more or less, as the adults around him/her expect. As fresh troops on the scene, my husband and I were able to approach our grandson with the expectation that he'd cooperate, be pleasant, and have fun. He rapidly and gratefully fell in line with this plan. He and his parents had briefly gotten into a vicious cycle of anticipating negative reactions from one another.

I well remember when this daughter was the same age. She and I were having a similar power struggle. The wonderful intervention of preschool melted the problem as though it had never existed.

A month after Christmas Eve, our children and grandson visited at our home. My daughter is in her second trimester and thankfully past the worst of her nausea. My son-in-law is back to being his solicitous and patient self. And, my grandson's peaceful face and relaxed demeanor proved that he's worked through his confusion and distress over the changes in his life. Whew!

Best of all, Dramma and Drappa came through the hazardous time without disillusioning their daughter, disorienting their grandson, or distancing their son-in-law. I consider it my best Christmas gift of the year, and one that overwhelms me with gratitude. Published March 2001

Gratitude

Rowan and Moira as Harry Potter and a lion for Halloween—three years after the story.

I LOVE YOU

Sometimes, I treat myself by telling everyone I pass, as I drive or walk, that I love them. "I love you, guy on bicycle." "I love you, family playing in the park." "I love you, homeless guy." "I love you, small or large, noisy or quiet dog." (I'm not saying this so they can hear me, but I am usually looking at them with a smile.) By the time, I have I-love-youed several, I can't wipe the smile off my face. This is an especially good practice if I'm going to a situation that has proved difficult or where I fear that.

Treat yourself. This practice is better than eating fudge sundaes—yummy, satisfying. I often have noted that, even when I'm in a car passing by quickly, some people/animals seem to sense someone has reached out to them. Especially children and animals (birds, dogs, squirrels, cats) turn to look directly at me—return a smile or look lighter and happier.

THANK YOU

Here's another treat as good—maybe better than—the "Good Things" lists that were the start of my gratitude journals, where I recorded my thanks.

My thanks categories might give you ideas for those people and things you can be grateful for, or perhaps just reading effusive gratefulness will be like a bath in warm fuzzies. Oh, and feel free to take any of these thank yous and apply them to yourself. I'm sure you deserve to be thanked for many of these types of behaviors or traits. Help yourself to a heaping handful of any of these and know that I know you're doing it...and deserving to do it. Here goes.

Deepest and most humble thanks for all those who have participated in allowing me to have a wonderfully enjoyable creative career: Thank you readers, thank you students, thank you clients, thank you publishers, thank you editors, thank you agents, thank you employers. Thank you any and all who have contributed money, favors, barter, compliments, opportunities, jobs, or anything else that has made it possible for me to have this great career of writing, editing, and teaching.

Thank you too husbands one, two, and three as well as a non-husband partner who also helped support me for a while in the indulgence I call my passion, my career.

Thank you my children and grandchildren for allowing me the time to write, edit, and work during your growing years. Thank you all for never yet telling me this was a bad choice or that you resented the time these things took. Thank you my pets and plants and homes and cars for supporting my efforts, for the company and comfort...the patience with my busyness.

Thank you all my friends, family, and writer pals for your feedback and support. In the competitive world of publishing, you have been integral to my success.

Thank you world of publishing...you fabulously interesting and generous world where I've typically been met with such kindness and openhanded sharing. Thank you editors and publishers who've mentored me and awarded me promotions, praise, and generous remuneration and unbelievable perks like travel and meeting famous people. Thank you coworkers who befriended and cooperated.

Thank you students for your approval and appreciation, for teaching me with your reactions/needs/wants the right ways to have the most rewarding teaching experiences possible. Thank you other teachers, support staff, photographers, illustrators for all you've added to my work.

Thank you Mom and Sister for allowing me to use your artwork with my writing.

Thank you Dad and Brad for the unconditional love and faith in me, all the amazing physical exertions on my behalf...the moves you managed with your brawn and brains, the home repairs, the garden tending, the dragons decorating the walls of my life!

Thank you Aunts for participating in my education, for talking to me like a peer, for mentoring, and teaching by example. Thank you, Dorothy, for the gift of mastership of the flute. You most of all gave me music—an intimate and accomplished experience with it. Thank you Uncles for modeling how to have interesting and creative careers.

Thank you, my lifelong string of cats—comforters, loyal and self-sacrificing, able to change my mood, distract me with your antics and caresses. Thank you for your intuitive paws on my cramps and stomach aches, the precise back walking on muscle spasms, the concerned looks into my teary eyes, the purring and kneading. Thank you my beloved dogs—precious companions, endlessly committed to our relationship—

Boots at my bedside, Decca on the farm, Tikah house guardian and devoted hand maiden, AJ sweet always present cuddler, and Aladar—constant friend and escort.

Thank you God and universe and to whom it may concern. My life has been and is one of joy and enjoyment, learning, survival, spiritual growth, awe, and pleasure.

Thank you trees and flowers, grass and sky…mountains, lakes, oceans, rivers. Thank you all the interesting places I've visited and the people who made those trips pleasant, entertaining, abundantly educative.

Thank you teachers and mentors…such time and patience you've lavished on me. In this, especially, I feel humbled and grateful. Thank you for caring, thank you for sharing, thank you for believing in me, trusting me with tasks even I wasn't sure I could accomplish. Thank you for not resenting times when I was too young to understand how much you were giving.

Thank you doctors, nurses, healers, techs and all those who have extended your hands and hearts at times when I was injured or ill. I am touched by your attention and caring. I am aware of your sacrifices and kindnesses. I know you have materially added to my ability to live with comfort and function. (Especially, John Bastyr, Mindy Wendt, and Alan Munk.)

Thank you Mom and Dad for the atypical childhood and college curriculum you turned our daily lives into. Thanks for all the reading and gentle hand stroking, Grandma. Thanks for all the lap sitting and oral storytelling with colored pencil illustrations, Grandpa. Thanks for the tremendous West Seattle home with view and hard wood floors, Grandpa John. Thanks for raising my father to be interesting, Grandma Muriel. Though I never met you, I feel you through the photos and stories and in my father.

Thanks for the parties—Christmas, Thanksgiving, 4th of July—

Don and Audrey. Thanks for including me in your life and trip, Dorothy and Leon. Thanks for playing with me, your older cousin, Kristi, and sharing your parents. Thanks for all the walks and the songs and the meals, Grandma Pearl. Thanks for the exquisite woodworked furniture and decorations, Grandpa Everett. Thanks for the carved Icelandic boxes, Uncle Leon.

Thanks mother-in-laws for turning out some uber cute and sweet men for me to wed. Thanks for training me in cooking, design, sewing, farming, parenting, and how to get along with a mother-in-law. Thank you all too for your generous and loving gifts. Thanks for being mothers to me.

Thank you, Mom for your mothering, all the conversations, the ever-changing and fascinating house and life in it...the decorations, the projects, the skills sets—sewing, reading, writing, teaching, cooking (pies, bread, pressure cooker meals, lebkuchen, eat-your-way-across-the-street pudding), home-making, parenting, animal care.

Thank you, Dad for your fathering—the unconditional love, the bizarre and fascinating adventures to numerous churches and other religious/philosophical/spiritual places. Thanks for the skill sets—exercising, yoga, carpentry, plumbing, boating, swimming, climbing, biking, driving, gardening, harvesting, cooking—weird weird stuff but so fun—chocolate covered ants, sardine sandwiches, stir fries, sprouts from all kinds of seeds, juices made of...everything!

Thank you, Sister for our days in the crib creating a twin language, for the nighttime cuddles and the car games we invented to spin away the time. For the stories you encouraged me to invent, for a lifetime of artwork I've gotten to watch you create, for the times you've stood by me, for the reminiscing together, for the sharing of health and living tips, for our nights sleeping in Hootenanny (a back building we turned into a clubhouse), for popcorn in the loft at Halloween, for wanting "Tiger" which I got for you and always count that as a BIG GIFT that I was able to buy. Thanks for years of phone calls and parties, for sharing the same parents and early life.

Thank you, Kristi daughter. Thank you for the wonder of my pregnancy and birth. Wow...turning during labor to present perfectly. Thank you for being my mama-loving baby, patting my back, defending me whether I ran that stop sign or not. Thank you for the ecstasy of seeing life's big moments all over again through a baby's eyes— holidays, travel to the ocean beaches, pets, school, coloring, dancing, learning to ride a bike. Thank you for being my constant companion in your young years...trips to Vancouver and Hawaii. Oh, we had some fun. Thank you for putting up with your mother's exotic little life...more than one husband, many homes, different schools for you. Thank you for being so gracious about that at the time and still. Still my defender, even defending me to me. Thank you for demonstrating your joy in riding, your persistence in getting that into your life, your hard work ethic, your generosity to me in every way. Thank you for having my elegant grandchildren Rowan and Moira and bringing them to live close by. Thank you for letting me spend time with them at your home and in my home. Thank you for the meals you've prepared for us, for the food and clothes you've lavished on me and on Brad. Thank you for your kindness and humor and loyalty and toughness. You are exactly right for me. Exactly my special package from heaven formed just for me, and this is always how I've felt and still. Thank you for listening to my struggles, for taking my side, for finding or trying to find solutions or ways to help.

Thank you Julie step-daughter...first of your sisters to live with your father and me. Thank you for your smiles and laughter, your hugs and sweetness, all the conversations. I embrace your being into my heart when I think of you. Thank you for wanting me back when your dad and I broke up temporarily; you came with dancing eyes to me and took my hands in glad welcome. That was a big moment for me. Thank you. Thank you too for Angela—my little angel girl who wrote the sweet thank you letter, for Lyle the boisterous and Charlie the thoughtful.

Thank you Connie step-daughter...second to arrive. Thank you for being my friend when that was the right time and relationship for us. Thank you for listening and loving and welcoming me back after your father's death. Thanks for joining in household building—taking classes at the college where I was going, swimming as a family, listening to books being read, watching television with us. Thank you for sweet forgiveness and inattention to my weaknesses that reminds me of my biological child. Friend you are and will be. Thank you for your strength and kindness and for sweet Lena, Laura, Josh, Chastity, Michayla, Hannah, and their lovely children...the wonder of great grand children. Thank you for supporting me, reading and reviewing my books...above and beyond the usual in friend or family.

Thank you Tracy, first to welcome me when I met your father, first to treat me like a mother. Braiding my hair as we drove on a trip. That was a big moment for me. Thank you. Thank you for your optimistic bombastic fun-loving antics. Thank you for our faxing follies— still keeping connection after I left. Thank you for finding me when your father died and letting me know. Thank you for the rib crushing hug when we finally got to see each other again ;-) Your energy and warmth make me smile whenever you come to my mind. Thank you too for being this stable, strong girl that has found her way to some of the best solutions in her life. Thank you for Christa and Isaac. Though I haven't met them, grandchildren still.

Thank you daughters, four. Thank you for getting along so well. For being this amazing fun estrogenic, "table of women" as Michayla so correctly named it. What a great gift this gaggle of girls, home full of females was for me. It was a bountifully beautiful thing to have and I am still thankful for the memories of it.

More thanks fill my mind, more things to say to each of my husbands, to boyfriends who made me feel attractive and took me fun places, to girlfriends who were delightful companions, to teachers, to the physical world for all its glories and comforts, to food—for Pete's sake ;-) I just made a pear pie...gratitude for that, indeed!

Thanks to weather, to timings that usually end up in my favor—just making it in time, or missing something that could have been bad...the avalanche we missed as Bill and I drank an extra cup of cocoa in our convertible. We would have been killed. Thank you angels of timing or eerie intuitions.

Thank you me for putting up with all I've put you through. Ha ha, I say, but yes, I'm grateful the patient loving part of me manages to tolerate and love into a better place the unhappy, jealous, fearful, or angry parts.

Thank you body for all the fun! Thanks for playing the flute so well, for swimming, for being such a whiz at sex, for being funny ;-) Thanks for working so hard to stay healthy and to return to health after injuries or illnesses. Thanks, and I really mean this, thanks for putting up with times I haven't treated you well enough, led you to places that were perilous or overused you just because I could. Thank you for the current 66.7 years, and thanks for all the others to come.

Thank you brain and intuition for finding good solutions and sussing out situations and people, for knowing things I had no way of knowing. For allowing me to follow a path beyond thought that serves me well. For bringing grace and light and joy and peace into my life. For recognizing Roth and Releasing and Jordan, and being smart enough or in tune enough to pursue those right and supportive ways to believe and practice.

Thank you spirit or soul for coming back again to the world to learn and evolve. Thank you for carrying me through the rapids of life. Thank you for leading me to the peaceful place. Thank you for all you experienced in previous incarnations. Thank you for your patience.

THANKS GIVEN TO ME

Here are some further examples of giving thanks. I have been the blessed beneficiary of much wonderful praise. These pieces show some different methods for expressing thanks.

Dear Ariele, This is my 8th book and I still have several more in the hopper. I love to write! I am glad that my readers enjoy my stories, my travel adventures, and my fiction. Writing has given me huge pleasure over the years and has allowed me to find my voice.

This is a gift you gave to me. Thank you so much for your teaching, your editing, your advice, and your encouragement. This book (*What Makes Me Happy*) is just one fruit of your good teaching. A car accident turned into a creative expression. I hope you enjoy. Janice Van Cleve

Hi Ariele! First of all I want to say I'm completely humbled by being in your class. I've taken many classes through the years and I feel the most connected in yours. You memorized everyone's names, you remember our stories, you're attentive and give great feedback. I almost feel like I don't deserve to be in your class so I hope it's OK that I stay. Lol! Anyway, thank you. Brian Ford

Hey Ariele~ Thanks for the article. I looked it over and am really honored that you chose to write about it for *Barefoot Running*. You are an amazing writer. I will go over it and publish it next week! Abbie

A poem for you, Ariele
Her voice is her garment,
words and sounds weave texture and color,
cascading, flowing, swirling, worn, wielded,
wrapping, holding, trailing,
beauty, grace, rage—
Calm as a queen in her robes.
Frieda Kirk

Dear Ariele, Thank you so much for sending me a copy of the July/August issue of *Northwest Prime Time* and for returning my pictures. Our Activities Director cut out my poem about our white cat and mounted it on our bulletin board for all the residents who might otherwise miss it to see. I was quite the celebrity for a week or so. Bobbie Peterson

Subject: thank you for being you

You're a treasure, Ariele. Such wisdom you've acquired and, by the hard way—living through adversity—but maybe that is how wisdom is garnered for most people, if they are going to evolve. Elizabeth Lyon

Ariele—You are such a kind & generous soul. Thank you for offering to do this. Thank you also for the note that you sent. I greatly thank you for your kind words. You are an amazing soul, and I feel blessed to have you at our center. You bring a sunny and loving energy to us and I am grateful. Have a wonderful week. Emily at Greenwood Senior Center

Ariele: Wow. Thank you for sharing this. I've read it probably ten times. The vulnerability in your writing moved me and gave me permission to feel some things that I have been blocking for a long time. I actually felt my anxiety level drop, just from allowing myself to relate. From a reader's perspective, I can see your strength and, thereby, find compassion for myself. Kathy Reeves

Dear Ariele, I have been following your column, Writing Corner, for a while now. I appreciate the work you do and always enjoy reading your advice. A few years ago, I moved from Seattle to Japan, but my lovely Grandma, who lives in Des Moines, has continued to send me regular clippings from your column. In one of her last letters, she included a piece from your Poetry Corner. Being a fan of your work, I wanted to send in a poem I wrote last year. Thanks for your columns. Elliott Hindman

Hello, all—We are being featured in an article about women's centers in the September edition of *seattlewoman magazine*. Big thanks to our Lifelong Learning teacher Ariele Huff for writing the article, and to all of you for providing good information!

Best regards, Cara Mathison, Development Director, UW Women's Center

Thank you Ariele, I am always surprised when you want to share my writing. My cheeks once again are hurting from smiling all day. Thank you for the encouragement. I continue to be happy I was guided to you. Hugs from April Ryan

Ariele, Wow! Wow! Wow! You did a lot of work and I loved your editing. I was nodding to myself in agreement and chuckling as I read your corrections. Fantastic! I will fix it and try to add some more emotional feeling that I now see it is crying out for. I'll send you the 200 word or less shirtail when it is complete. Thanks!!!! Susan
P.S. Ariele, I realized my writing was emotionally two-dimensional while your suggestions for improvement were a vivid 3-D!

OH MY GOD... Ariele, I am falling off my chair (and it's a barstool so I have a long way to go to hit the floor—yowza). Thank you SO much. I am grateful beyond words [for your MFA application letter of recommendation]. Thanks again, Sandy Dentremont

Hi Ariele, I just want to pay you a compliment. I have taken part in a writing class at Edmonds CC and although the material and the preparations of the teacher are excellent, I am missing the personal involvement, the lively interchanges, the discussions "and what did you think of this?"—in short, your unique way of getting the students into the heart of the matter, of sharing experiences and sometimes baring their souls. Keep up the good work, Manfred Reimann

Ariele M. Huff

Amazon.com eBooks authored by Ariele M. Huff

Making Mud Angels: Winning Strategies in ToughTimes
http://www.amazon.com/dp/B00S0JD7M6 Need a fresh start? Help is here. Achieve success when finances, diet, health, or relationships are troubled. Easy Action Plans are gifts from tried and true wisdoms of the ages. Join the fun path to a better life. Paperback: http://www.amazon.com/dp/1507617070

KITTEN LOVE: http://www.amazon.com/dp/B00OOHB068 Three kittens in a box under a bush. What was I to do but take them home? In this game changing choice, I've learned a lot about myself, my husband, our two elderly pets, and how a single moment can make your life over --whether you wanted that or not! It's a raucous ride with melting moments and unbelievably adorable kittens. Plus, a couple of bumbling pet owners hoping to survive their best intentions. HELP!

Learn from My Mistakes   http://www.amazon.com/dp/B00PLQNU0K An open diary of the happy, healing, humorous adventure—exploring obstacles and discovering solutions--bringing three abandoned kittens into our lives!

Crazy Cat Ladies and why we do that This is the story of how my husband and I graduated from lifetime owners of one-cat-at-a-time to Crazy Cat Ladies and why we love it so much. The answer is NOT what you think it is!
http://www.amazon.com/dp/B00V975HKG

Fifty Shades of Graying: Love, Romance, and Sex After Fifty
http://www.amazon.com/dp/B00T85X2T4   The result of a blog where people shared stories, essays, & poems on the topics.

The Perks of Aging: Blessings, Silver Linings, & Convenient Half Truths eBook: http://www.amazon.com/dp/B00VFAFAAE

Paper back: https://www.createspace.com/5399818

The Queen of Mean: The Conversion of a Cold and Prejudiced Heart
http://www.amazon.com/dp/B00TMCFPBG

A tattoo appears and comes to life, shocking a bitter bureaucrat with letters in her own handwriting and nightly out-of-body travel. True stories from immigrants and refugees mingle with folktales and myths in a book that shows how spirits can bring magical change—whether you want it or not! Fantasy novella.

Paperback: https://www.createspace.com/5408791

The Successful Risk Taker
http://www.amazon.com/dp/B00Y7PT366
What makes one person more prone to be a daredevil than another one? Why riding the risky but fun roller coaster, pushing limits, and love of adventure add up to the good life. A diary of childhood secrets and adult results. Roll the dice and win!

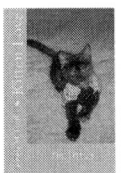
Kitten Love: The Trilogy The rescue of three fragile kittens, abandoned in a park. Their first months documented in three books, now forming a trilogy of touching, hectic, and illuminating journals of tiny lives...and the people and other pets affected by them. Challenges and lessons in love.
http://www.amazon.com/dp/B0167GEGFA
Paperback: https://www.createspace.com/5602517

Get Rich, $tay Rich Make money your friend and servant. Learn the simple ways to becoming the richest person you know. This easy workbook is a step-by-step guide to bettering your life and your circumstances. Wealth is within your grasp.

http://www.amazon.com/dp/B012W5Z2W6 Also in paperback

Housekeeping Anthology of essays about householding gathered since 1999.

Funny and unexpectedly revealing.

http://www.amazon.com/dp/B01B3M4KW2 Also in paperback.

The Soloists Like child actors and athletes, musical child prodigies often pay a heavy price for their stardom. The people are real. All the  situations and most of the events are real. This narrative nonfiction is written in novel form to document the lives of children placed into often brutal adult level competition, taking readers through the resulting emotional consequences. With a main character composited from two real life soloists, this novel is written by a family member.

https://www.amazon.com/dp/B01FNY5TO4

ABOUT THE AUTHOR

Ariele Huff hosts a website segment—Sharing Stories—on the LOCAL page of *Northwest Prime Time*. Contact:
http://northwestprimetime.com

Columns Writing Corner and Poetry Corner are in the print version of *NW Prime Time* which is free at libraries and senior centers in Seattle and surrounding areas. Send your stories or poems for Sharing Stories or Poetry Corner to ariele@comcast.net.

Website for writers: http://arielewriter.myfreesites.net
Blog: http://writerswingsbyariele.blogspot.com/
Blog: http://fiftyshadesofgraying.blogspot.com/

Made in the USA
Middletown, DE
20 June 2016